The Mistress of Longing

WENDY HAVLIR CHERRY

WOMANCRAFT PUBLISHING

Published by Womancraft Publishing, 2019
www.womancraftpublishing.com

ISBN 978-1-910559-51-2
Also available in ebook format: ISBN 978-1-910559-50-5

Cover art by Lisbeth Cheever-Gessaman

Cover and interior design by Lucent Word, Cork, Ireland.

Praise for *The Mistress of Longing*

The Mistress of Longing is a mystic's portal into a sumptuous dimension of Life we can all access. It is our sacred invitation to embrace, embody and dance with our longing.

The Mistress of Longing not only provides permission for all our longings and desires but holds them as the sacred doorway to our belonging. I found myself taking it in like manna from heaven. It's truly a pure, potent and powerful transmission of Divine Truth. I experienced cascades of sensation in my body as my heart and soul were being awakened by the Mistress of Longing. I wanted to devour the book whole but recognized the need to slow down and pace myself to fully receive and metabolize its wisdom.

This book is a welcome new resource for me. I will to return to it again and again – in part or whole – for deep nourishment, guidance and support.

**Joni Advent Maher, creator of the
Trust Your Sacred Feminine Flow podcast**

The Mistress of Longing is like the fragrance and softness of rose petals offered to our collective hearts. It is a deep invitation to live in and with our longing and to offer the poetry of ourselves again and again. Wendy Havlir Cherry speaks directly to the Soul and whispers to our fear and hesitation, beckoning us to live the fullness of ourselves. She not only inspires but also offers concrete, potent exercises to help guide our journey. Don't miss this bounty.

Heidi Rose Robbins, The Radiance Project podcast

Wendy Havlir Cherry delivers lyrical lines coupled with sharp insights that speak to the way we connect to ourselves and one another with a deft and dazzling hand.

Briana Saussy, author of *Making Magic:*
Weaving Together the Everyday and the Extraordinary

The Mistress of Longing is a beautiful beckoning to open to a wisdom that guides us to reach, to connect, and to create. In a world that often numbs us to our impulses and desires, The Mistress of Longing lovingly calls us back to the center of ourselves, challenging us to rise with passion and courage to claim our birthright to thrive rather than merely survive.

Amy Bammel Wilding, author of *Wild & Wise*

The Mistress of Longing is a creative breath of fresh air. It inspires me to listen to my inner stirrings, and reminds me that my wildest, most beautiful visions – along with the next steps to bring them to fruition – are within me, just waiting to be discovered, if I carve out the time and space to listen.

Katie Hess, author of *Flowerevolution: Blooming into*
Your Full Potential with the Magic of Flowers

Wendy Havlir Cherry will entice you and invite you to enter into 'the forest of awakening' that lies inside your heart. "It is lush and green and wooded with wildness." In The Mistress of Longing, Wendy opens a world we rarely see expressed – the world of the sensuous, creative, succulent feminine.

It can be hard to put words to the feminine principle. As mystery herself, She defies definition. Wendy, though, writes from the heart, truly from this forest of awakening. Allow yourself to be enticed into the world of She.

Julie Daley, CPCC, innovation catalyst, transformational leadership coach

In The Mistress of Longing, Wendy Havlir Cherry transports us on the power of her dream to our tender hidden desires. This heartfelt and heart-fueled book leads us into a meditation on what we truly want, and how we truly deserve what serves our greatest good. I could see this book as a joyful guidebook for women's groups who might focus on one chapter each time they meet. The poem will be an entrée into deep conversations and heart openings. Line by line, women have the opportunity to see their truest hearts' longings to belong. There is such gentleness here!

Gina Martin, author of *Sisters of the Solstice Moon*, Book One in the 'When She Wakes' series

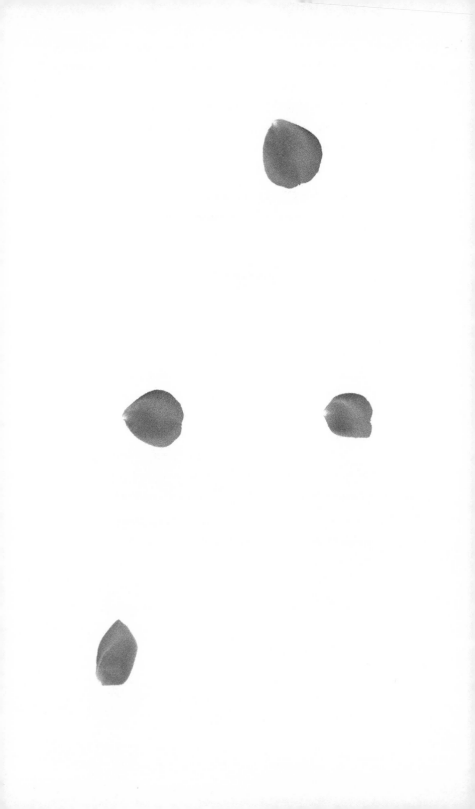

Foreword

As a publisher I work in service to our authors, the creative source, their joint creation and the world, facilitating connection between them. In the course of this work there are magical moments when a book comes along with such a strong life of its own that it is quivering.

This is such a book.

Deceptively small.

It contains real magic.

When I first read the manuscript of *The Mistress of Longing*, I realized that I had entered a process. Or rather the process had entered me. The soul of the work, its cover, the way it needed to be shared, those we needed to approach for endorsement all appeared in my mind's eye. All that was required from me was to trust the process and say yes. I get this experience to some degree with the majority of our books. With *The Mistress of Longing* it was incredible… like plugging directly into Source. Our first author-publisher call was unusual to say the least, there was no doubt to either of us that the Mistress of Longing was in attendance, and had enabled the whole process. Our conversation started with the words "You're beautiful," and continued quickly into mutual tears of a shared heart connection.

As an author my personal fascination is in giving voice to lost archetypes of the Feminine. I am so deeply grateful to Wendy for introducing me to an archetype of the Feminine that has always been there, but remained nameless. Allowing the voice of the Mistress of Longing to come through her is a profound act of service.

What I need to tell you is that *The Mistress of Longing* is true and real. She is not made up. You do not need to believe in her. When you open this book you open a portal to a direct energetic transmission – can you let your heart and mind receive this possibility?

Simply allow the words on the page to begin your remembering.

Take a deep breath in.

The Mistress of Longing is here. For you.

Throwing rose petals at your feet in blessing,

Lucy H. Pearce

Don't hold back
Be the face of the earth
This is creativity
I want to show you
Light me.

The Butter Lamp

*L*ast March, on the Spring Equinox, I received a poem while I was sleeping.

I have received many poems over the years during the Dreamtime. Usually, I am able to capture themes, images, and other nuances of my dreams that then become poems.

But this poem was different.

It kept humming through my dreams, word for word, until I woke up. It was the invitation to write this book. Although I didn't know it at the time.

All I really understood was that a butter lamp was the author of the poem. And the Butter Lamp was intent on getting me out of bed that night.

When I wrote the words down, I was fascinated.

I was also confused.

I wasn't sure what – *be the face of the earth* – meant.

I did know, however, deep inside my bones, that I had been holding back and the time to emerge into my life in a new and different way had come.

I also remembered that years ago, a friend had given me a butter lamp that she had brought back from India. This butter lamp had been sitting on an altar of mine ever since.

But I had never used it for light.

I felt this dream, this poem, was telling me something about how to understand the light. And so, this poem became a sort of mystery that I put inside the pocket of my heart, trusting that at some point, I would understand its message more clearly.

I placed the butter lamp on an altar in my office, and made a practice of lighting it every day. This became a gesture of my devotion to being shown, just as the poem instructed.

About six months later, another poem came.

This was the second occasion that an entire poem was delivered to me in my sleep, word for word. At first, I resisted. I was tired, it was deep into the night, and the bed was so warm and soft.

But the author of the poem was fiercely insistent, chanting the words over me again and again, until I couldn't help but wake up.

Opening my eyes, I was filled with longing.

I longed to know what it wanted from me. What it wanted to tell me. And that desire to know made it effortless once my feet hit the floor.

In the dark of the night, I got out of bed and padded down the stairs to my office. I turned on a light and typed the words out on my computer.

When I saw what emerged, I knew that something incredibly special was happening. I had an immediate sense that it was more than a poem. I understood there was something bigger in mind.

The words from my dream – I am the Mistress of Longing – became a mantra that awakened something deep inside me. It is as if I became inscribed with poetic lines of truth inside my veins, all emerging from numinous layers of ancient wisdom that permeate the luminous experience of life.

They became like keys, unlocking door after door of new insights.

These words have changed my life profoundly. Waking me up in so many ways, not just out of a sleeping, dream-state. This includes the awareness that these words are not just about me, but also about you, and everything that is wanting us.

The process of receiving the words, my willingness to trust them, and the source they came from, was an initiation like nothing else I have ever known.

I began to get curious about the voice behind these words, and discovered that there was so much more she wanted us to know… about Her… about ourselves… about each other.

Over the previous year, I had known there was a book inside me waiting to be written. I had a felt sense of knowing this. It was like I was pregnant. I waited and waited to know what the book was about.

I tried to make the book happen at one point, because I was starting to think I was crazy with this notion of knowing that I was "pregnant with a book." But it didn't work. It felt odd and awkward every time I approached it and I became more and more resistant to the process of writing it.

Until the poem arrived I had no idea what the book was to be about. People would ask, and I would say I had no idea. But I knew. I just knew. I can't explain it any other way. Something was growing inside of me.

Imagine the magic and excitement I felt when I finally understood what, exactly, was asking to be born! For the month of September I simply sat with the knowing that the poem was the book. But I was a bit afraid and didn't do anything with it.

Things started shifting, though, one day in late September when I asked for help to write the book during my daily devotional practice. That night, I found the person who would help me give birth to the book by actually taking steps to bring it into form.

It was like magic.

The process of writing the book has been nothing short of awe and wonder, gratitude and love. The process of being with its author has humbled and changed my life.

I know that this book is for you. It is for all of us. It is a love letter to awaken your soul. It is a map that can guide you into your heart root: the place where your true knowing and all that you long for resides.

At a time when we need more love, more joy, amidst the incredible disbelief and shocking transformation occurring daily, She is here like a treasure map to lead us into a new frontier of hope, expansion, and sacred revolution.

We are being called to create a new way of being present with challenge, along with a new way of being present with joy. We are being called to understand the meaning of harmony, generosity, and profound compassion for all beings, everywhere.

I believe that the words on these pages are here to help give birth to more compassionate ways of living. These words will reveal and remind us that we are already whole and equipped to handle challenge and loss, fear and desire in ways that encourage more ease and grace not just for ourselves, but for the benefit of humanity.

This is a time when we need to carry the wisdom of what matters most: our connection to the vast unknown, and to each other.

O n the following pages, you will find the poem that came for all of us that night in September. You will unlock the teachings of each stanza, as given to me by the Mistress of Longing, She who is the true author of the poem. You will also receive clear steps and ways of working with this information in the last chapter.

Whether you read the book all the way through from start to finish, or simply open the book daily, trusting your hands will turn to the page you need in that moment, I know you will fall madly in love with the heartbeat of your life.

It is time to not only know, but to practice, our empowerment.

We need more hallelujahs.

May these teachings liberate your joy.

May you know that you are sacred.

May you share your gifts and light with the world.

And may we all be free.

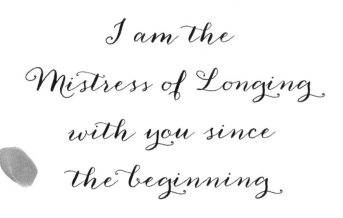

I am the
Mistress of Longing
with you since
the beginning

*T*he Mistress of Longing has been with us since before our first breath. She was with us as we came crying into this world, longing for the safety and warmth that we had known for nine months tucked away in our mother's womb. Her presence is constant hospitality, consistently available for our benefit.

She is different than God or a deity. She is the self-governing, self-determining freedom built into our essence. She is the midwife of creativity. She is the embodiment of desire. She is the sensation of longing that propels you to move closer to what you love. She is whole and holy. She is sweetness here to empower your love and your sovereign nature. She is an internal guide within and a powerful ally from beyond.

She is the first breath and the last breath. She is all the breaths in between.

Every inhale is a desire for life. Every exhale a desire for release and rest.

Dynamic energy and then rest.

Dynamic energy and then rest.

Have you ever noticed the pause right between the end of an exhale and the beginning of an inhale? She is there, too. She is the wind-force wisdom that bridges the cycles of being, over and over again.

Our longing is a dynamic energy as rich and necessary as breathing. It keeps us here until our final breath, at which point, She blesses us on our way to the next destination.

She loves our longing. She protects and blesses our longings with sanctuary.

Imagine a wave encircling you right now.

That is belonging: an invisible skin holding the essence of who you really are.

That is Her.

What would it be like if you knew you were never alone?

How could you walk through your life?

What would you do with the treasure of each breath?

What pleasures would you embrace?

What hardness might feel softer?

A few years ago, while I was working at a residential treatment center, I began to understand the sanity of addiction. At its core is longing, which is our natural state.

Addiction, the way I have experienced it, both in my own life and with those I have worked with and those I love, is a pattern of repetitive actions that are harmful to our essence. And yet, we reach for them because they bring some sense of relief.

It is my belief that desiring relief is a whole and holy desire.

While facilitating mindfulness and storytelling groups, I saw over and over again how this reach itself is the medicine. What we are reaching for isn't always the best option. But the reach itself is an intrinsic knowing to belong to safety, nourishment, and a clear, strong, enduring center.

I found that I began telling my clients that their reach was a whole and holy action, toward something that exists underneath what they were actually reaching for. Underneath the alcohol, drugs, or sex addiction, was the desire to feel safe, at home, and at ease.

The Dalai Lama has said that we all want the same thing. We all want to be happy. We all want to experience less suffering and more ease. We are born fresh out of our warm and cozy mother cave and into the stark, cold, harsh light with the longing to feel less discomfort and get to safety.

The Mistress of Longing is here to tell us she is right here, available to and for us. She desires to lead us to our belonging and that which will help us experience the truth of who we already are.

There is radiance in your longing.

Inside the longing is vast potential, lifeforce, healing, sexual energy, sensuality, intelligence, creativity, wisdom, love, and compassion. In these first two lines of the poem, the Mistress of Longing introduces herself to us and also tells us She has been here all along. When we feel vulnerable and unsafe, She is there. When we feel comfort and at home with life, She is there, too.

*Y*ou might already be considering in what ways you feel at home.
In what ways do you feel safe, nurtured, and well-fed?

In what ways do you not?

What longings do you have that connect you to a desire to feel safe, nurtured, and woven into a family or community of loved ones, warm and at home in your life?

We often look outside of ourselves for belonging. Forgetting that home can be found in our own bodies. And this is a vital place to start.

Take a moment now if you like, put the book down and stand up. Just feel your feet on the ground. Take a moment to become aware of your big toes, the balls and heels of your feet.

Take a few deep breaths and begin to stretch in whatever way it feels good. Just let your body and your breath lead the way.

Maybe include some neck and shoulder rolls, stretch your arms up toward the sky, bend over and just hang.

How do you feel in your body now?

What other ways might you be able to feel a sense
of groundedness, safety, and warmth?

Perhaps a cup of hot tea and a blanket might feel really good.

Or a walk in the sunshine, a hot bath with nice rose petals and essential oil.

Or a piece of dark chocolate melting slowly in your mouth.

Notice what longings might be present, as well.

Remember that the Mistress of Longing is your constant companion, she has been with you all along.

She is ready and waiting to help you come home to your true belonging.

I am the invitation
and your hands
opening the envelope

*W*e came equipped to long, and to belong.

Often, we long for what we perceive we do not have. And yet if we long for it, it is living inside of us. This is the wisdom that comes over and over again from our desire to create.

Longing and belonging is the impetus of the creative cycle.

The creative cycle begins typically with some desire to bring something into form that isn't currently. We begin to engage with what that is, and how it can come into being. In short, we begin to get curious about it.

Then we begin to actually "make." We make and make until finally, we have created something we can see, know, understand and feel. We ride the waves of that creation until it drops off into a sense of nothingness.

Afterwards there comes a pause, a space where we do not create. And this repeats over and over again.

This is as it should be.

When we are in the creative process, we are working both with what we long for and with what we've got.

Our bodies know this cycle well.

Our sexual energy is the same.

We have a desire, a physical longing to express through our body. We might begin by simply entertaining the idea, contemplating it, getting curious about what we desire.

Then we begin to move our bodies closer to another person, or perhaps with ourselves, making physical contact and creating through the senses, taking in what feels good, giving and receiving, until we reach the climax of the experience.

The energy subsides. Spaciousness begins to unfold again.

We rest inside this until the next wave of creativity rolls in.

Our desire is the invitation. And, we are also the envelope being opened. Our hands and bodies are both artist and muse.

We are all of these things.

We are all the juicy parts of the creative process.

When desire arises, it is a message from our pleasure center. When we allow ourselves to listen and be present, much delight can result. Whether we are trying to write a book, carve a sculpture, build a home, make love, or collaborate a vision with others. The rising force of desire is a powerful one.

This is belonging to our longing with fierce devotion.

We are meant to create.

Creative energy is life energy. Our very lifeforce.

This is why it is essential that we pay attention to our desires. Our desire is the wanting of life. The wanting to be here. The impulse to live and thrive.

How beautiful is that feeling?

Sexual desire is the impulse to create. It is simple, elegant, and necessary.

We can understand sexual desire as a sort of storehouse of energy, which when aroused can move up and out into the rest of our life until we reach a point of pleasure and fullness.

We can look at our creative endeavors and notice an incredibly similar process.

> *What happens when we block the flow through our thoughts or beliefs that it isn't okay to create?*
>
> *What happens when we know it is and we move with the process?*

The Mistress of Longing wants us to understand that desire is like a love letter to our life.

Our desire is sacred, whole, and holy. We honor who we are when we receive the invitation, open it and participate in the process of creating.

*P*lay is a creative act, and a very sacred one.

When we are little, often the creative part of ourselves gets belittled or pushed away for safety and survival. Eventually we stop playing.

If you notice that it is challenging to be playful or to be with your creativity, you might look back to what happened when you played or created when you were a child.

Our bodies store these memories.

If it's safest to stay away from our creativity, we will.

The only problem is that at some point, our lifeforce begins to wither away because it isn't being renewed, restored, nourished.

Intimacy can feel the same way.

Because intimacy is a creative act.

It takes curiosity, openness, and playfulness to create with another person, to be in our body in an exploratory way.

> *If creativity is sacred, how can we invite in*
> *our longing so that we can belong to it?*

We cannot belong if we do not first open ourselves to being opened.

We can become attuned to our bodies, to the energy and area where desire is longing for sexual expression.

We can re-member our ability to open with self-compassion, and honor the vital lifeforce that we are and that wants us to be free.

This might be something we need to ask for help and support with. Maybe we need to spend time with a counselor or healer to do this. Or maybe simply increasing our own awareness will decrease the hesitancy and obstacles to let our creativity fly free.

The most important message here is to begin to build a compassionate relationship with our desire and with our creativity. It is the key that will unlock every other door of our lives.

Question anything and anyone who tries to tamp down your creative spirit, your desire to thrive, and your longing to make love to your life in all the ways you can.

Remember, it's okay to belong to your longing.

The Mistress of Longing highly recommends it.

As do I.

You are the envelope and the hands opening it. Do so with fierce and unwavering devotion.

Our desires aren't just about us. Their energy is of benefit to us all. The urge to live carries us all and moves us forward.

Light permeates light.

The recipe for love is love.

Longing finds homecoming in belonging.

We are meant to consciously carry the impulse and spread the light like a woven tapestry throughout our inner and outer worlds.

If we stop wanting to create, be it art or new political dynamics, a beautiful meal, a robust relationship or healing process, then we wither away. This can lead to feeling trapped and uninspired, ending committed partnerships that otherwise could thrive, or political systems that go unchecked.

A radical way to practice social and political activism is to create. Let that energy and desire move through you and offer it to the world.

Don't wait for perfection. There is no such thing.

Your desire is more beautiful than you might know.

You are sacred.

We need you.

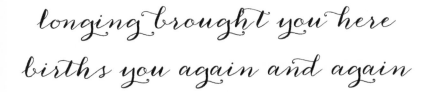

longing brought you here
births you again and again

*L*onging not only brought you here, but gives birth to you again and again.

Just like each new inhale, every new longing can infuse us with lifeforce. The Mistress of Longing really wants to emphasize this: we are continually renewed and rebirthed throughout our lives. And desire has everything to do with it.

With each new breath, we become more of who we are.

It takes a lifetime.

To desire is to live.

To dream is to create.

To carry a vision with truth and confidence is to be a light bringer. It is possible to bring light into the darkness. We need more and more light.

Having the opportunity to be renewed over and over again isn't a miracle. It's our birthright.

A way to work with this is to trust in the longing and desire to be wanted, included, and to have purpose. These are natural, normal desires to have.

To know, through life experience, that challenging emotions do and will arise, frees us from the belief that we are doing something wrong. In fact, it can offer us more compassionate presence when we feel scared, directionless, confused, and alone.

This is a form of generosity that we can bring to simply being here.

It can be a huge boon, not just for how we are in our own lives, but also because it can allow us to tune into others' needs of not wanting to feel alone and scared. This can be an investment in the foundation of goodness in our lives as well as a renewed resource we can share with others. Embracing suffering as a natural part of life provides self-compassion for our own and empathy for others'. When we understand this inside ourselves, we are less critical and judgmental about good versus bad, right and wrong, pain and joy, and thus, available to apply generous doses of loving kindness. This is a practice we can engage with over and over again.

We can be inspired by the idea that every time a longing arises, new life and new opportunities can be the result. This is a truth that can nourish us deeply. For when we are attuned to our heart's deepest desires and gift ourselves accordingly, we know the regenerative lifeforce and healing of compassion that comes as a result. We can share this with others.

Longing is a sacred threshold that can lead to more beauty, understanding, inspiration, and generosity; this can and will impact entire communities and people all over the world.

Knowing that longing carries with it the possibility to live a heartful and generous life allows us to embody hope and a sustainable vision for the future.

It is time for us to remember the qualities of our belonging.

And to practice them daily.

I am the impulse to live
the threshold of
each new breath

*T*his is the willingness to show up and be with your life. Exactly as it is. To lean in with curiosity and devotion to what is arising. Reaching into what is possible inside the threshold of each new breath.

This is the inhale.

The embodied action to move, to meditate, to walk, to book the trip, to make love, take the chance, try the new recipe, call the friend, light the candle, sing the song, say the thing.

This is the desire and the embodiment of all of it.

This is moving beyond the dream and making it real.

The taking of your seat in the circle of belonging.

One of the things I have taken away from my training at Naropa is Chogyam Trungpa's words of wisdom suggesting that when we actually sit down to meditate, that is the act of a warrior. It takes great willingness to be present with one's self, with one's state of mind, with whatever level of humming is happening in one's body. To pay attention and be with.

This is the threshold of each new breath.

This is the discomfort.

The choice to be with completely, and not edit or try to change it in any way.

This is the natural inclination of the body to inhale again, after each exhale.

This is vibrant life.

Real life. Not always pretty, but definitely beautiful. Because it is the pulse inside the skin from the heart beating as a devoted consort of life.

This is the rising after a depression. The reach for the support that will help. This is the water you drink because you are thirsty.

This threshold of life is the energy of love made manifest, often invisible, but potentially always known.

This is where the truth of desire and the organic beat of

more life…

more life…

more life…

moves.

This is the wild tincture of possibility: birth, death, and everything in between.

The Mistress of Longing is asking us to be with the energy of our life now, pure and simple, to belong with how we are and what we have.

Being present is action implemented with intention and consciousness.

This is a bridging of mind, heart, and body toward emergence. This is like cleaning out the closet to appreciate the things we already have and let go of what we no longer want. This is sharing the wealth with others so that they, too, can experience abundance, warmth, and the feeling of having plenty.

The threshold of each new breath can be experienced in myriad ways. This is the uplift of energy that can carry us to our desired destination or whip us into oblivion depending on our presence with it.

The Mistress of Longing wants us to know that there is always a threshold of sacred wisdom to enter through.

Inside your heart is a door that leads to the forest of awakening.

It is lush and green and wooded with wildness. The kind that stirs the senses and encourages growth. Move deep into the forest and see what awaits you there, what instruction is given, what gifts are handed over to you to enjoy and delight in and share.

This is a journey that only you can make for yourself.

Find the time and take the journey. Don't just schedule it. Do it.

You only need five minutes to move across the threshold of your sacred sanctuary.

Light a candle, burn some incense, inhale the scent of pine, lavender, or rose.

Breathe.

Just be with your inhale and exhale.

Close your eyes.

In your mind's eye, picture a spiral staircase that moves from your mind down into your heart. Descend the staircase. You will find a warm fire inside the cave of your heart, with some comfy cushions, a pot of tea, and green crystals lining the walls. Just sit at the fire of your heart. See what or who comes while you are there.

Soak it in.

Ask for the next steps so that you can take action. Ask the spirit of your wisdom to come and sit with you and tell you a story.

Ask questions. Receive answers.

When you're finished, say thank you. Take a snapshot of your cave in your mind and return up the stairs to the present moment of your life.

Draw or write what you experienced.

Take the next step.

Be the embodiment of your desires.

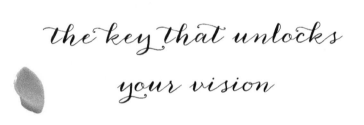

the key that unlocks

your vision

*I*s there a room inside you where all your longings and dreams are kept? Do you visit it often? Or do you walk by it and try not to look? Is it uncharted, locked up territory where you don't even dare to tread?

There are so many reasons why we resist our longings.

I wonder what yours is.

The Mistress of Longing wants us to know that this "room" is a sacred space that holds so much of what we are looking for.

She is the key to unlock your vision. She is the way to move safely over the threshold and begin to sift and sort, acknowledge, and be present with the yearnings that churn within.

Sometimes, just by acknowledging our longings, they begin to shift and transmute.

And sometimes not.

Often there is a conscious, active embracing that needs to be explored.

To do so is a whole and holy practice that will set something free inside of you.

Something powerful and big and game changing.

And perhaps that is why that door is locked for some of us. Perhaps it's just way too scary to go there because we have a sense it will upend life as we know it. But if this is true, the life we are living is too small for us.

There is freedom in the longing.

The Mistress of Longing is right here with us. She is the midwife that will cross the threshold with us into the scary, unknown places and help us emerge with more sanity, confidence and clear seeing.

It is only through entering our longing that we can also unlock the door of belonging.

The word 'longing' was first used in a geographical context. People who were far away from each other were said to be "long away." Belonging was to come together again in close proximity.

Therefore, we must come into close proximity with our longing so we can also belong.

Being the longing brings the truth in close, like not being able to see and then finding the right pair of glasses and being able to read the menu in a dark restaurant, becoming aware of all the options and possibilities. In fact, we can use longing to move deeper into passionate purpose. I'm not referring to the idea that there is one thing we are here to do and that if we don't find it and do it then we're not living our purpose. No, no. That can actually prevent us from living the truth that is unfolding right here and right now.

Passionate purpose is about living in the moment, feeling comfortable and warm in our skin, even amidst pain, fear, and uncertainty.

It's about living awake.

It's about living in the midst of all this discomfort and knowing we can bring blessings to the obstacles.

Most of us just want to experience ease, comfort, belonging and peace. These things can be our passionate purpose. We can bring these qualities into any and every experience, be it a dream job or one we hate, our relationship with ourselves and those we love, to our bodies, our choices, our movement, pauses, and everything in between.

If you long for love, that is your vision.

If you long for purpose, that is your vision.

If you long to live somewhere sunny and warm instead of cold and cloudy, that is your vision.

Our longings hold so much valuable data. When we give ourselves permission to acknowledge and be with them, we give ourselves permission to want what we want, and to take up space and feel. We allow ourselves to be genuine and true to our heart's desire.

This is a really good thing. We belong here. We do. Just because.

This also gives others permission to do the same.

Take down the sign that says, "Do not enter."

Take the key that the Mistress of Longing embodies and use it.

Use it to set yourself free.

This is your permission slip if you need one.

For many of us, we weren't taught that we can actually stay true to our own desires, wants, and hold boundaries if needed, while also expressing ourselves in a beneficial, liberating way. Instead we have learned to put others first, to use compassion for others, and abandon ourselves.

I beg you to apply heaping helpings of self-compassion like salve.

In the wise words of Yogi Bhajan, "if you cannot bless yourself, then nobody else can bless you."

One of my favorite stories in *Women Who Run with the Wolves* by Dr. Clarissa Pinkola Estés is "The Crescent Moon Bear." The main character is faced with some pretty big challenges and is told by the village healer that she must go on a journey to retrieve the hair of the Crescent Moon Bear. Along the way, she comes across many an obstacle. Every time she says *"arigato zaisho,"* which means

Thank you, path, for presenting me with these challenges,

Thank you, path, for removing them.

She is blessing her own path with these words throughout her entire journey.

I think this is very wise advice.

When we unlock the room where all of our dreams and hopes and desires live, we are blessing our own path. This is similar to speaking our truth and expressing what it is that we want. The key here relates to our ability to speak, sing, proclaim, express ourselves and what we need. To ask for what we want and be clear about what we don't want.

This is opening the door to belonging.

I have known so many women, and men, too, who have been taught to be quiet, sit still, repress, don't express. If truth were a room, it might be a restricted area, its door bolted up tightly and sealed. Perhaps we learned that we must abandon our own truth in order to be loved, accepted, safe even. But in the present, we can find ways to choose truth. We can unlock the longings and bring light and air and nourishment to them. We can express ourselves in so many ways. Through speech of course, but also writing, art, movement, and even, silence.

Knowing when and how to be silent when we're not used to it can be tricky at first but is a whole other language itself. We can find so much wisdom through the expression of silence.

Sometimes simply using our senses to "unlock our vision" is the way in. Feeling our feet as they come into contact with the earth, looking into someone's eyes as they share something with us and dropping everything else, smelling the intoxicating aroma of fresh bread baking, listening to the waves of the ocean, or feeling the warmth of the sun on our skin.

Noticing what feels good and what doesn't is radical these days, because it is wisdom that can only be unlocked from within.

Experiencing ourselves as we are will cultivate self-trust.

This is the ultimate key that the Mistress of Longing is asking us to hold onto and use.

I am the unfolding
of desire
soft opening

The unfolding of desire begins before we acknowledge our longing.

The seed of yearning is planted when a sense of spaciousness makes room for new arising. This is not so easy to put into words, because it has to do with the very creation of consciousness which is happening all the time.

We are creative essence, we can't help but make space for longing and that which we long for.

There is no clear demarcation of this opening because it is a simple arising of source energy that always was, always is, and always will be. From the time before we were planted as little human seeds inside our momma and well after we leave this world, creation itself is longing. It moves through the cycles of life and death, again and again. We are dynamic beings always in motion, always devoting ourselves to something, even when we are not aware of it.

Desire is a constant companion.

The Mistress of Longing is all of it.

She is the creative spark, the seed, the emergence, the dynamic experience of being, the beginning, the ending, and all the spaces in between.

Desire unfolding is the soft medicine leading us to a new reality of merging with the light of constant motion within – a life that can never end.

When we believe our longings will go unmet, we experience a sense of grief, loss, anger, and immense disappointment, perhaps even shame. But the Mistress of Longing tells us that she is the unfolding of desire. She is also the longing being met, and hence, the belonging.

How do we know that we are experiencing desire?

We feel it.

Something stirs within us.

Our bodies are wise.

Our minds can have stories about the longing, too, of course.

But our bodies have a direct and unfiltered experience of yearning.

The Mistress of Longing is the felt sensation of warmth inside our skin aching for something outside itself, the hollow belly hungry for food, or the grieving woman whose skin longs to feel the touch of her lover's hand again.

These longings are whole, organic, holy experiences that should not be taken lightly or judged as good or bad but instead known for exactly what they are: a soft opening creating space for belonging to happen, a way to know, in our bones, the essence of our lifeforce.

This is incredibly powerful. For if we didn't experience these real yearnings as signals or indicators for what we need and want, how else would we know to reach out, to find what we seek, to create and merge with what we love and belong to?

If this were not holy, why would we all experience it on a daily basis?

We do a lot of self-editing to make such longings go away. Because many of us were taught that to long for something shows fear, not enoughness, vulnerability, shame, and even grief. Any shade of grief is often eschewed in our culture. Especially by the powers that be. Discomfort is considered taboo and should be hidden.

Even the diagnostic manual that psychologists and psychiatrists use dictates what kind of grief is more or less "normal," and what isn't. After a certain amount of time, grief should disappear. We should "move on."

This is one of the many ways we are taught that life exactly as it is, is inherently bad. We should do whatever it takes to be youthful, and hence, valued. We should be happy. We should be successful and follow the rules set by the dominant culture. Strength and power come from aggression, intellect, and position, not rest, receptivity, or intuition. We should only love particular people and in particular ways.

Often, longing is right up there as something considered problematic. This is a very small lens to look through when exploring the expansiveness of the human experience.

Let yourself belong to what you love and long for.

This might be challenging as it contradicts what most of us have learned.

But the willingness to soften, to let in something more gentle and true to your unique experience is the opening.

This is holy ground, ceremony for the body, mind, heart, spirit, and soul.

When you long...

You open.

When you open, a soft space emerges to receive what you belong to. Much like a flower opening to a bee, a woman to her lover, a song to the voice that sings it. When we don't allow for this, judgment hardens the soft edges, and we can become less generous with our acceptance of self and others. Yet, there is an inherent knowing about love that exists inside us. Anything else is a story, created by an effort to suppress, oppress, and buy into some idea of safety.

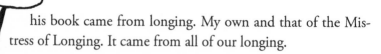

*T*his book came from longing. My own and that of the Mistress of Longing. It came from all of our longing.

Speaking with a client recently, she told me, her voice quivering through tears, that she just wanted the time and space to fall apart. She felt this wasn't allowed and she was supposed to "hold it all together" on a daily basis. This, dear reader, is a longing that all of us must heed, we must fall open.

To fall to our knees in grief, exhaustion, hopelessness, is the soft opening. Once there, we can meet ourselves in a new way, one that cleanses and restores us and begins to build something new while marking the end of something we have once known, be it a person, an experience, or a really tough day.

These moments are ritually important, they are food for the soul: nourishment for a life's journey. At the end of this book is an apothecary of ways to do this. You will find numerous options to help you move closer to your truth and to live with devotion. There is a path of sacred revolution and active revelation. You will find practical ways to bring this into your daily experience.

But for now, this soft opening is the beginning. Consider it like the entrance to the sacred mandala of your life.

Longing is the medicine that will lead you in.

Longing isn't just about a desire to make love, buy a car, or obtain the perfect job, although these things can certainly be a part of it. Longing happens in the wee hours of the night as we dream; in the morning when we hope to receive good news that day; in the desire to see the sunrise or a beloved's smile flash. Longing is the desire to have fresh clean sheets, or a hot meal on a cold day. Longing is the burning need to feel free. It is the desire that a loved one could stay longer in this life.

Longing is about making meaning out of our precious time here. It all matters. Every gesture. Every feeling.

Let the soft opening come. Everything you want matters.

You and your longings are more sacred than you know. Your confidence and sense of safety in life makes an impact upon our world. Ironically, that comes from softness. When we feel safe, we have the presence of mind to consider others. We know what grief is being suffered around us, and how we just might be able to help because of our own awakening, and because of our willingness to belong to life exactly as it is.

Please know that your life is meant to be lived right now, not when you lose the five pounds, or finally land the job, leave or get the relationship, get enough follows on Instagram, or ace the exam.

If you are waiting, ask yourself, what is it that I believe I will be available for or will make me matter more when it happens? Because darling, that is your longing. That is what matters now.

Let yourself belong to that.

Now.

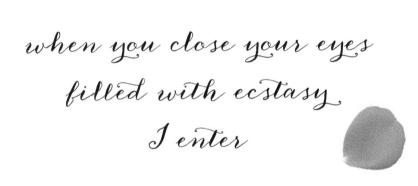

when you close your eyes
filled with ecstasy
I enter

When you close your eyes filled with ecstasy, the Mistress of Longing enters, to infuse you with the understanding of the immensity that you are. Your pleasure is possible.

You do not need to purchase anything or hire someone to make this happen. You are the maker. You are so much more than you know. This can happen right here, right now.

These words are meant to bring hope.

Much like the North Star, they arrive at this time so you know that there is guidance available to you and that you can receive that guidance.

You were born immense. You were born of the light and with the light. You are the light.

When you close your eyes filled with ecstasy, this is the time you can access true knowing, through the delight of your beloved body. This is your truth.

The mind is trained to banish this knowing. But your body will never lie. She aches to remember this truth. Because there is an inner ember aglow and delight is the sacred wind that moves it throughout the body into luminous truth.

It doesn't matter if you believe your body is imperfect. For the divine cannot be changed no matter the form. If you are young or old, scarred or unblemished, round and curvy, or slim and athletic, this matters not. For your body is whole and holy. You, beloved, are whole and holy.

In ecstasy, we remember.

This is a soul knowing released through the exquisite pleasure of being in a body. The softening that comes through the portal of flesh and bone is grace. This grace becomes an elixir infused through our veins and deep down into the tiny sparkles of our bones, our etheric fields, and into the velvet of our intrinsic nature.

The Mistress of Longing is the infusion of remembering. Much like a match that lights the fire, She reveals that sacredness is our intrinsic nature. There is nothing that can change that. Through our howls and moans, sighs and presence with the body, we merge with this knowing. The Sacred becomes our embodied experience rather than an untapped source. The faucet is always there and we must turn it on to receive the water.

We were designed this way.

The Mistress of Longing wants us to remember this truth of ourselves. When we do so individually, we provide the mirror that gives others the information to do the same. This is our divine right and that is why She has come. To help us gather this grace and to tap into the unlimited nature we already are. She wants us to know how deeply She longs to enter. We are not alone.

This can happen sexually, of course. We can enjoy this gift by giving it to ourselves or by being with another. This can happen sensually, with a juicy peach dripping down our fingers or the moist sweetness of a freshly baked slice of chocolate cake. This can happen listening to the sound of a waterfall. This can happen as our body rhythmically moves to a salsa song or the beat of a simple drum. Or by taking our shoes off in the forest and letting the soles of our feet sink into the damp, dark earth. Even looking at a photograph of a beautiful place or someone special can bring about this ecstatic feeling of awe.

Your wonder is soft strength. When a rainbow appears and you stop everything to take it in, that is the Mistress of Longing infusing you with hope and trust in something wonderful. She brings the proof. She comes in this way to activate the sacred imprint of who we are. Let yourself feel the warm touch of skin against yours by someone you love. Receive the beauty around you. Really take a moment to be with that beauty. Close your eyes and imagine a place you love that is sanctuary. Let it fill you. Let it become you.

This can also be true when we howl with grief on some level. There is something otherworldly that pierces us, the intensity of feeling, the deep, deep reach for relief can provide an odd but exquisite return home to our true nature.

When we ache, when we yearn, when we are filled with delight, something transforms inside of us. We become more fully ourselves.

Remember, it is the Mistress of Longing calling you home to yourself. To your divine truth. There is nothing else you need. Only your body and your willingness to soften and let Her enter.

You are so much more than you know.

The Mistress of Longing tells me this all the time. These eight words have become a sacred mantra She pours into me daily. She pours through me so that you will know, too. Perhaps you already know but have forgotten. This is your reminder.

Think of a time now when you had an experience of softening and opening. Let it come flooding back inside of you. Close your eyes. Who were you with? Where were you? How did you feel? What did your senses experience? Take some time to drop into this memory. Float inside it. What knowing comes? Let the ecstasy pour over you, into every cell. Take your time.

When you have finished this process, write it down, draw it, or move it. Mark it as sacred remembering. Build an altar to it in some way.

Do not forget it.

Invite more of it to come into your life now. Because this is your medicine, and your medicine will be a balm for us all.

I am the windbreath
that pinkens your soul

*L*ast night, as I was sleeping, I dreamed the Mistress of Longing was showing me that my body was a holy gate, and that the erotic gesture of opening, softening my limbs and my need to control, is the portal for the windbreath to move through and pinken my soul.

I became an altar, a gesture of poetic discovery and illumination. I became an expansion of delight.

Of course she would share this with me on the night before I write this chapter to make sure I really get the picture. And so, here it is, dear reader. It is the energy of wanting creative source to have us, completely. This comes while opening and letting go to the softness of our wild nature. It is the experience of orgasm that radiates the light within, spreading like warm wildflower honey throughout our being. It is a rich and explosive ceremony that marks the pinnacle of our existence.

The explosion of hormones during orgasm awakens us. It expands our consciousness and quickens the numinous lifeforce within and around us during this amazing process that we have so cleverly been designed to experience. Not just once, but many, many times throughout the course of our lives.

Orgasm is a celebration of our life exactly as it is. There is no concern about extra layers of fat, or the look on our face, or fearing we don't look the way we think we should look or be, for that matter. It is the freedom in letting it all go and trusting in the desire we feel. Giving ourselves over to the sheer pleasure we are capable of. We become lost, in some way, to the intensity of feeling oh so amazing inside our skin.

To be clear, the Mistress of Longing also shares that orgasm is not the only way to be with the windbreath. It is both metaphorical and literal. The windbreath pinkens our soul in the final process of any creative act. It is the big release, the giving birth. It is the making of something that was once only an idea or longing into a physical manifestation of celebration. It is in many ways the enlightenment of life that we are capable of because we are in this human body.

To know the soul in this way has always been available to us. But perhaps we haven't understood it this way.

There are those who have seen the body as a temple, as holy ground. The ethereal sense of something bigger happening all at once during orgasm is in many ways indescribable and often ungraspable and yet, it is what brings a slight ray of pink to the soul of our time here. It is what moves the hands to spin the clay and mold something beautiful to share.

The pinkness does not yearn to be grasped. It is merely a luminous quality arising for a time that cannot be boxed or defined but simply felt somehow inside the skin, reflected through the mirror of our lover's eyes, or perhaps "seen" by the heart. And although it is not the goal here, it is a sacred, floating destination to be enjoyed when it comes.

This can be experienced during the exchanging of vows, during the final touches of an art piece or written work, the handshake at a life changing business agreement, or while giving birth to a child. It isn't an ordinary experience. It is the marking of something beyond what drives us to make and create, that happens along our journey here. It is inspiration to not only create but complete. It is, in some way, the "evidence" of our triumph. The victory at the end of a challenge. The coin to mark sobriety or the hallelujah when the call finally comes through. Or the willingness to say yes instead of no.

It is the proof in the pudding. That all along something or someone has been listening, most especially ourselves, and this is the answer, the most deeply soulful desired outcome. The belonging showing itself to the longing.

It can feel dreamlike or awe-some because often we can't quite hold onto it. Because it is the known yet ungraspable light that slips away before we want it to. But it will leave the door ajar for more. Often, we might not be able to take a picture of it. But it will be imprinted in the heartroot of our existence. The code that changes our language and relationship to life as we know it.

Devotion is the key to unlocking the truths of our longing. Devotion is a daily opportunity to experience belonging and to softly, softly open ourselves to the possibility of being pinkened by the wind-breath, again and again. It is behind the reach for "just one more drink," for more things, more sugar, more lovers, more intoxication for whatever it is we are afraid to feel. It is the essence inside the essence. It is worthy of our attention and will ultimately lead to the pinkening of our soul more than once, if we let it.

The Mistress of Longing walks with us in so many ways and at all times. From the beginning to the apparent end, and then some.

She whispers now to you...

What would you do if you knew
this were true? How would you
belong to your desperation? How
would you set out to find me?
What fears might you set aside to
acknowledge that you are not alone?
What might you pray for? Say yes to?
What soulful pleasures would
you give yourself to?
What would you devote yourself to?

leave rose petals at the gate

I will come

*T*his is the last line of the poem that came from the Mistress of Longing. Reading these words now, six months later as I write this last chapter, I am humbled. I am so grateful that She woke me up in the middle of the night insisting I put her words on paper. I cannot express how grateful I am that you are holding this book in your hands right now.

"Leave rose petals at the gate I will come," is a crucial and beautiful instruction; a way for us to move forward toward our (be)longing. This is putting into action all that we have dreamed, contemplated, and desired. This is an exquisite opening of fierce trust and surrender. This is a call to making it real: a sacred revolution, a daily devotion.

Interestingly, the instruction was to write this chapter first. This, for me, is telling about just how important our taking action and making our hopes and vision real, really are.

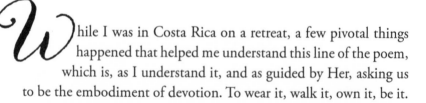

*W*hile I was in Costa Rica on a retreat, a few pivotal things happened that helped me understand this line of the poem, which is, as I understand it, and as guided by Her, asking us to be the embodiment of devotion. To wear it, walk it, own it, be it.

One morning during the retreat, we were invited to think about something that we were feeling challenged by. Then, we were guided to move beyond just the thinking. We were invited to take that experience or feeling and embody it in a pose; to find a way to make it real by fully becoming it via the vessel of our body.

My challenge, as I perceived it that day, was the pattern of being hijacked by fear, specifically, the fear of not being good enough or worthy of receiving what I longed for. I felt trapped inside it, and yet, somehow it was safe, shielding me from vulnerability and being exposed for my "not enoughness." This fear was what had held me back from fully stepping into my true self, as Beauty Gatherer, a title given to me in a dream, when I first returned to Santa Fe after living in Colorado for many years.

To embody this, I started from a standing position. My body knew exactly how to be with this fear. I bent over and hugged my legs tightly, leaning a bit to the left, with my head and face tucked under, hidden, unable to be seen. It took tremendous energy to stay in that pose. I was using every muscle to stay there. Every muscle in my face, jaw and neck were tight. My body was trying to keep up with this attempt to control everything in and around me. I felt afraid of taking up too much space, unsafe, and actively frozen, closed off, stuck, imprisoned.

We were invited to deepen the pose, to really lean into it, feel it, and give it everything we had in order to exaggerate the feelings, sensations, and understand ourselves in this way more fully. Interestingly, later, we shared our poses in small groups. I watched someone else move into their pose which was strikingly similar to mine (because how many women struggle with a sense of being stuck, small, not free to move in the direction they long to, to take up more space?) I was able to see myself in a way that even being in the pose didn't allow.

What was fascinating about this was that I remembered a dream that came to me long ago that I didn't quite understand. Until right then. Being in my body, witnessing another doing the same, was an untethering of information that had been in a holding position. This is why taking the steps to embody who we are and what we belong to is the medicine of our time: it gives others the opportunity to see something similar, so their own truth can be actualized.

In my dream, I was in a grocery store crouched down into the almost identical pose, as a way to shield myself. Something had happened somewhere in the store, a loud, threatening sound, perhaps gunfire. As I was tightly crouched down and balled up, I felt the presence of something. I looked up toward my left shoulder and a bald eagle was perched there, her right eye looking directly into my left. This dream felt real. I was in awe of that eye looking directly into me.

Today, I understand this dream as a gift of eagle vision, showing me where and how to focus my attention, especially when I am feeling small and scared. Eagle can be seen as the great communicator of the Divine, who sees all things with a spacious perspective.

We are made of all the elements; earth, wind, fire, water…and the space in between them. When we make contact with all of these elements living inside of us, a fresh perspective can breathe through us. I believe, too, that the eagle wanted me to know that I wasn't alone. None of us are. We are never alone.

There are many ways to know and remember this. Sometimes, the Dreamtime comes as an awakener of truth. Often, it comes through being present with what is. This is the underlying message of the Mistress of Longing and the love song she is singing for all of us.

When this information became available because of this exercise, I had a visceral reaction. More became unbound inside of me. I knew I was integrating new, healing information. The next step of the embodiment practice was for us to let our bodies guide us into a pose that represented the exact opposite of the challenge we were experiencing. Just as my body knew exactly how to get into the fear pose, she knew exactly how to get out of it and embody fierce trust and openness. Much like the eagle showing me how to see from a spacious vantage point, I unfolded effortlessly into a standing position, knees slightly bent, my heart open wide, shoulders back, eyes closed and face looking toward the sky. I became open, courageous, trusting, and in love with possibility.

Devotion is an act of sacred surrender.

It is not failure or submission. It's the willingness to be present and available to life in this moment.

When we leave rose petals at the gate, we are in essence saying, "I accept and honor you," to ourselves, and to life, exactly as it is. We are actively and intentionally opening ourselves to receive our own true nature. We are saying, "I am open to wanting what wants me."

No closed posture has space for this kind of generosity. When we are closed, we are protected, but only for a time. If we stay closed, we can begin to shut down, becoming less available to possibility and the wonder waiting for us.

At some point, we can realize that empowerment comes from our ability to let go, to stop trying to control, to release the tight-fisted grasping. When we are open, we can receive. There is a softening that happens that infuses us with integrity, authenticity, and power. Within that softness is great strength.

Take One Step Toward Me

Another profound experience I had during the same trip was going to the ocean. Something in me was afraid to go. I was afraid of my softness, of my almost fifty-year-old body being seen. I felt exposed and vulnerable. That's pretty challenging when you've been hiding for so long.

But once there, I was so drawn to be near the water. All of the sudden, innocence came forward along with awe and wonder. I yearned to be part of the beauty I was seeing all around me. And I'm not sure I knew it then, but I also yearned for the beauty living inside me.

I wasn't expecting this, but as it happened, my body automatically began to soften. I let my body lead me. I could feel my facial muscles relax and my heart open. Because I was writing daily to the Mistress of Longing for this book, it seemed She was with me, taking me by the hand, saying, *Come now, let's go.*

The magic of the ocean was waking something up inside of me.

I took off my sandals and made my way to the water. I remember feeling a bit giddy, excited, and like my actions were deliberate and *on purpose*. My face felt like a beacon of light. My smile was so wide. I felt free in a way I hadn't in such a long time. When my feet felt the sand, I let go. I let go of everything, including worry, and fear. I was completely present. I was madly in love with the soul of my life loving me. I knew in my bones, the water was the Mistress of Longing, The Boundless Source of Everything.

She immediately came toward me. I felt my entire life of devotion being met by the spirit of the ocean. Her water gently caressed my feet. I felt Her say, *Here you are.*

She kept telling me,

Take one step toward me and I will move toward you.

I felt Her longing for me. Like She had been waiting for me to confirm all my desires, whispering into the pores of my skin,

I'm right here.

My stepping toward Her was leaving rose petals at the gate.

To this day, when I think back to this moment, I become it.

I'm not sure I can ever articulate what happened for me that day, really. All I know is that remembering brings tears of homecoming every single time.

Take one step towards me, has become my daily instruction. It is, for me, the answer to any challenge I can and will experience in this precious and fleeting, human life.

Leaving rose petals at the gate is the invitation for all of us to experience this. We become the scribe, the invitation, and the knower.

Now is the time for all of us to experience something like this, each of us in our own way, of course. Because it will open us to a radical new way of being that brings inner peace and a still center when everything around us is whirling chaos.

When we are in our true center, we become a generous helper for others. I'm sure I don't have to tell you, we need more generosity in our world. We need more peace and new ways of being. We need new ways of taking action, honoring differences, and creating the kind of change that will inspire inclusion, shared resources, and a sustainable vision. We need compassionate leadership that leads to less hate and more love.

Our devotion is our vote in motion. What do we actively choose? We hold great power to make a difference in our own lives, in our communities, and in our shared world.

Now is the time to remember that there is a force, an energy, an ally waiting for you, for all of us. The thing is, we can't receive the ally's gifts unless we soften, open, and prepare ourselves to receive.

You don't have to buy a plane ticket to the ocean. You can find your feet right now and see in what direction they want to move.

What is the gate of your life and how is it leading you home to your devotion? What is the entry place or sacred threshold where your light lives? Where do your helpers, Creator, spirits, angels, whatever you call them, reside? How can you take one step, make one small gesture to offer yourself to their wisdom and love?

What's holding you back? What obstacles are in your way?

The obstacle is also a sacred threshold. Leave rose petals there, as well.

A deep softening strength comes when doing this. And the more we do it, the quicker we can remember that our longing leads to belonging. Our muscle memory, our senses, our skin, remember. But so too does our spirit, which loves being closer to soul in this way. This can be a way of fine-tuning the light to come in. Like using your own vessel; your mind, heart, body, spirit, and soul, to be the tarot spread, the pendulum, the oracle.

You are sacred.

You are the oracle.

Your body, heart, and mind have limitless ways to access this wisdom, this restoration of spirit.

Finally, the Mistress of Longing wants to remind you, there is no separation.

Your body, your essence, your being is the gate.

You are the altar where all wisdom and love already resides. And your actions, every gesture, an offering.

You are longed for.

Find a way to let your longing know you are open to receiving.

Just one step will do.

More Rose Petals...

$\mathcal{M}$y time with the Mistress of Longing has been like being inside a wild apothecary. There are dried flowers and herbs hanging from the rafters, glass bottles of tinctures, flower elixirs of all kinds dressed in beautiful colors, and the walls, ceiling, and floors smell of old, oiled sacred spice, from trees that once anointed the earth. Our visits are like prescriptions.

Since she first started coming in my dreams and now, each day when I sit down to write, I am changing. Not into something new but back into myself. She has told me, over and over again, this medicine is not just for me. It is for you, too, dear reader.

With tears cleansing my eyes now, I ask you to open to this knowing. I invite you into the apothecary of our time. Simply be with your knowing. I trust these words have come for you at the just right time.

$\mathcal{A}$s I was completing what I thought was the last chapter, I asked if there was anything else She wanted us to know. She offered many, many more words. This chapter comes as an offering. These final words are a loving gesture.

The Mistress of Longing wants us all to know what is available and longing for us.

She is stepping toward you because in reading, you've been stepping toward Her, over and over again with the turn of every page. She shares the medicine She has gathered over time and space, bringing it here for us now, to embody the true and generous sweetness we are.

She wants us to do whatever we can to expand our minds even more and actualize the abundant belonging of who we are.

*F*irst, the practice of simply quieting our minds at least once a day, and asking for guidance is something she wants for all of us.

This will build trust in ourselves and our own inner knowing which She says we need to strengthen. This will also cultivate deep relationship with Her or whomever it is you wish to ask, be it Spirit, Creator, Mother Earth, the Divine Feminine, a guide or helper.

*T*he Mistress of Longing says,

Prayer or song, a quiet whisper, or a
river of tears, all beckon me to your side.

Tarot or a pendulum are also
ways of calling to me.

I can help you experience and
trust your own intuition.

Journals are altars.

Card spreads are altars.

Creative processes are altars.

These are gates,

the entryway into the highest self,

to the wisdom keeper that lives within.

Practicing gratitude is essential. It is nectar for our mind and body. This will influence our lives dramatically, helping us experience our wholeness. Science is proving this again and again. Gratitude is another way to leave rose petals at the gate and will alleviate great suffering. Whether you find a journal you love and write a few things daily, or simply think about what you feel grateful for when you rise in the morning and go to sleep at night, you will know more calm, clarity, and resilience.

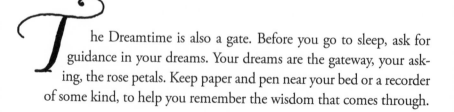

The Dreamtime is also a gate. Before you go to sleep, ask for guidance in your dreams. Your dreams are the gateway, your asking, the rose petals. Keep paper and pen near your bed or a recorder of some kind, to help you remember the wisdom that comes through.

The Mistress of Longing longs to hear about our dreams and visions. She says that our dreams and desires beckon Her to come and be by our side.

Remember I want to be near you.

Just like the ocean waiting for your feet,

I want to know your hopes,

dreams, and aspirations.

This is how you can call for me.

Build an altar to what you love.

What belongs on that altar? What can you feed the altar? Some water, a candle, a stone or crystal, some words? These things could encompass all of the elements: earth, water, wind, fire, and space. You could place an offering of sweetness, too, like some chocolate, or a little jar of honey.

*I*s there a tree where you live that you feel drawn to? An area of interesting stones and rocks? You could leave an offering there, in nature, too. Preferably one that will decompose naturally over time. You could sit near a river or stream, any body of water, and just breathe.

Let your breath be aspirations you send out to the water, to be carried onward into the world and back to you.

The heartroot of all of this is the crystal clear luminosity that burns brightly in the center of us. This is ceremony.

Ceremony is happening all the time.

*L*eave a love note for your longing.

Breathe. She will come.

You are a vast ocean of experiences, desires, hopes, loss, beauty, fear, and love.

You are an altar, worthy of love.

The Mistress of Longing wants us all to know that we belong to love.

When we are holding grief in our hands, we still belong to love.

That's why we long for it.

*T*ake a moment now to create some space to write down, speak, sing, dance, or embody in some way, your biggest challenge (you could do the embodiment exercise I mentioned earlier, for instance). After you've taken some time to center yourself and breathe, simply write down a question or worry on one side of the paper, then on the other side, begin to write and see what answers come.

What does your fear or challenge look like, sound like,
taste like, feel like? Lean toward it. Back away if you need
to. Then try moving a bit closer again with curiosity.

What do you see? What does this challenge really want now?

How can you write or embody that?

If nothing was holding you back, what
would you live, say, and do?

How and who would you be?

*A*nything rose is also helpful to help you connect to Her.

A warm bath sprinkled with rose petals or sipping a cup of hot rose tea are both beautiful ways to rest into self-compassion and understand the loving quality of longing and nurturing of the heart. Using rose quartz or taking a rose flower elixir. If possible, growing roses just outside your front door or in your garden can promote a magical reminder of rose's essence and healing powers. If you can't grow roses, visiting a rose garden is just as sumptuous and good for the heart.

Studies have shown that even looking at an image of roses provides similar healing benefits. These practices will only multiply and create ripples of love out into the world, to the farthest reaches of humankind. And we all benefit from that.

The Mistress of Longing has a very long list of all the ways we can leave rose petals at the gate. She suggests while engaging in these things we simply think of Her.

Light a candle.

Say a prayer.

Write a poem.

Make a wish, write it down.
Place it somewhere special.

Leave an offering.

Create a vision board.

Go to the park and swing.

Walk toward what you love.

Ask for help.

Put your body in water and open.

Lie on the earth and open.

Let yourself weep.

Fall to your knees.

Dance.

Make art.

Make love.

Eat cake.

Do something that brings you pleasure.

Color with crayons.

Talk to a flower.

Hold something you love.

Leave a note of kindness on
someone's car just because.

Think of someone who needs help
or encouragement and imagine
that you are giving it to them.

Recently, the Mistress of Longing taught me that I can close my eyes and draw the medicine of the earth up through my feet and all the way up through my body. The light from above is also available, and can be brought down through my crown chakra and body. Coming together at the heart center, I am healed, energized, a lighthouse. She is teaching me that this can be done at any time.

Bringing the light in, in this way, is a way of leaving rose petals at the gate. It's a way to let the light come to you, She says.

Whatever you do, do it with love and a willingness to soften. That is when the Mistress of Longing will be near you, guiding you, showing you the way.

Right now, She is waiting.

This belonging is a co-creative act. A sacred collaboration. So many of us have forgotten. But we are not alone. Ever. Radiant support is always waiting near.

Finally, the Mistress wants you to know that you are the gate and the rose petals. There is no separation between us. Your body, your essence, your being is the gate. The altar where all wisdom and love already resides. And your actions, every gesture, an offering.

She wants you to know that as you read these last words now, She is here.

She will still be with you once you close the book.

She wants you to remember.

Mistress of Longing Poem

I am the Mistress of Longing
with you since the beginning
I am the invitation and your
hands opening the envelope
longing brought you here
births you again and again
I am the impulse to live
the threshold of each new breath
the key that unlocks your vision
I am the unfolding of desire
soft opening
when you close your eyes
filled with ecstasy
I enter
I am the windbreath that
pinkens your soul
leave rose petals at the gate
I will come.

Acknowledgments

I would like to thank my guides for unlocking the doors and leading the way. The Butter Lamp for her sacred instruction and generosity. My husband for his incomparable love, endless enthusiasm, and honoring. Julie Daley for her soulful support, divine timing, and encouragement. And Womancraft Publishing for believing in the messages contained in this book.

Of course, I want to express my profound gratitude to the Mistress of Longing for her boundless devotion and unwavering companionship.

And for you, reading this now, thank you.

About the Author

Wendy Havlir Cherry is a poet, teacher, spiritual mentor, and mindfulness instructor. She holds two Master's degrees from St. John's College in Eastern Classics and Sanskrit and Liberal Arts, and a third Master's from Naropa University in Counseling and Contemplative Psychotherapy.

Wendy has worked for many years as a psychotherapist with individuals and groups to uncover, reclaim and empower their inner wisdom and deep, intuitive knowing. She is a long-time student of Dr. Clarissa Pinkola Estés, PhD, mysticism, and devotional poetry. She offers individual guidance and group teachings, combining her professional expertise with esoteric wisdom and life experience grounded in practical devotion and daily practices, including meditation, guided visualization, altar building, sacred space creation, poetry, ritual, the intuitive arts and storytelling.

She lives in Santa Fe, New Mexico, with her husband and their beloved canine, Roland The Great.

This is her second book. Her first is *The Reach is (W)holy; Poetry Inspired by the Sacred*, published in 2017.

SHEGATHERSBEAUTY.COM

About the Artist

*L*isbeth Cheever-Gessaman is a visual artist that merges technology with traditional mediums to create new interpretations which serve as spiritual offerings and prayers to the Divine.

Using a flexible range of tangible media across a wide range of surfaces and contexts, the work produced is a union of the creative all-soul which explores shamanic and mythological constructs by incorporating art and talisman to create a (third) phenomena, or magical reality. This augmentation of discrete phenomena is dedicated to the celebration of the holy feminine, and an offering of beauty and praise to the sacred, invisible world that gives us life.

She is the illustrator of "The Divine Feminine Oracle," "The Spell-casting Oracle," and "The Sutras of Unspeakable Joy" by Meggan Watterson. She creates and lives in the eclectic mountain town of Manitou Springs, CO.

SHEWHOISART.COM

About
Womancraft Publishing

Womancraft Publishing was founded in 2014 on the revolutionary vision that women and words can change the world. We act as midwife to transformational women's words that have the power to challenge, inspire, heal and speak to the silenced aspects of ourselves.

The Womancraft community is growing internationally year on year, seeding red tents, book groups, women's circles, ceremonies and classes that honor the Feminine.

We are the change we want to see in this world.

Join the mailing list for samples of all our new titles, plus exclusive pre-order offers, discounts and Womancraft news.

WOMANCRAFTPUBLISHING.COM

And join the community on social media.

(f) womancraftpublishing

(🐦) womancraftbooks

(📷) womancraft_publishing

CREATRIX: SHE WHO MAKES
Lucy H. Pearce

"*C*reatrix is a more accessible identity for us to claim, especially as women, than the archetype of Artist, which has been forged in the male image for so long.

"To live as a creatrix is to dedicate your life to nurturing and sharing your creative gifts, using them in every way you can to imbue the world with greater colour, beauty, joy, understanding, playfulness, daring, rebellion…"

From bestselling author of *The Rainbow Way* and *Burning Woman*, Lucy H. Pearce, comes *Creatrix: she who makes* – a soul-full companion for the road less-travelled, to support the life that unfolds when we say YES to The Creative Way.

This definitive guide covers vast territory, from owning our creative gifts and our voices, claiming space and time to create, the dynamics of the creative process, to the key parts of Creative Entrepreneurship from marketing to building soul-led communities.

Featuring the lived wisdom of dozens of creatrixes from around the world, including: singer-songwriter Eleanor Brown; artist Lucy Pierce; sculptress and author Molly Remer; doll maker Laura Whalen and many more.

WILD & WISE: SACRED FEMININE MEDITATIONS FOR WOMEN'S CIRCLES AND PERSONAL AWAKENING

Amy Bammel Wilding

The stunning debut by Amy Bammel Wilding is not merely a collection of guided meditations, but a potent tool for personal and global transformation. The meditations beckon you to explore the powerful realm of symbolism and archetypes, inviting you to access your wild and wise inner knowing.

Suitable for reflective reading or to facilitate healing and empowerment for women who gather in red tents, moon lodges, women's circles and ceremonies.

> *This rich resource is an answer to "what can we do to go deeper?" that many in circles want to know.*
> **Jean Shinoda Bolen, MD**

THE OTHER SIDE OF THE RIVER: STORIES OF WOMEN, WATER AND THE WORLD

Eila Kundrie Carrico

Rooted in rivers, inspired by wetlands, sources and tributaries, this book weaves its path between the banks of memory and story, from Florida to Kyoto, storm-ravaged New Orleans to London, via San Francisco and Ghana. We navigate through flood and drought to confront the place of wildness in the age of technology. A deep searching into the ways we become dammed and how we recover fluidity. A journey through memory and time, personal and shared landscapes to discover the source, the flow and the deltas of women and water.

> *An instant classic for the new paradigm.*
> **Lucia Chiavola Birnbaum, award-winning author and Professor Emeritus**

BURNING WOMAN

Lucy H. Pearce

A breath-taking and controversial woman's journey through history – personal and cultural – on a quest to find and free her own power.

Uncompromising and all-encompassing, Pearce uncovers the archetype of the Burning Women of days gone by – Joan of Arc and the witch trials, through to the way women are burned today in cyber bullying, acid attacks, shaming and burnout, fearlessly examining the roots of Feminine power – what it is, how it has been controlled, and why it needs to be unleashed on the world in our modern Burning Times.

> *A must-read for all women! A life-changing book that fills the reader with a burning passion and desire for change.*
>
> **Glennie Kindred, author of *Earth Wisdom***

Lightning Source UK Ltd.
Milton Keynes UK
UKHW011250110621
385340UK00001B/22